HOW THEY LIVED

A TEENAGER IN THE SIXTIES

MIRIAM MOSS

Illustrated by
Mark Bergin

HOW THEY LIVED

Editors: Alastair Jervis and Elizabeth Clark

First published in 1987 by
Wayland (Publishers) Limited
61 Western Road, Hove
East Sussex BN3 1JD, England

© Copyright 1987 Wayland (Publishers) Limited

British Library Cataloguing in Publication Data
Moss, Miriam
A teenager in the sixties. – (How they lived)
1. Great Britain – Social life and customs –
1945 – – Juvenile literature
I. Title   II. Series
941.085′6   DA589.4

ISBN 0–85078–977–X

Typeset by Kalligraphics Limited, Redhill, Surrey
Printed and bound in Belgium by Casterman S.A.

CONTENTS

THE SWINGING SIXTIES

It was Whitsun Bank Holiday. Jackie's elder brother, Dave, had already left on his Lambretta scooter for a day out in Brighton. Jackie had wanted to go too but Dave had said she was too young, being only fifteen.

Instead, she was going round to her friend's house to listen to records. In the afternoon they planned to take the bus into London to visit Carnaby Street.

Jackie pulled on her purple mini-skirt and pink 'skinny-rib' jumper. Her knee-length boots were under a pile of Beatles posters. She pulled them on and sat down at her dressing table. She backcombed her dark hair, put on her eyeliner and smoothed on some white lipstick.

The latest number-one record was sitting on top of her portable Dansette hi-fi. It was 'Have I the Right?' by The Honeycombs. Jackie picked it up, ran downstairs and out of the house, slamming the front door behind her.

The year is 1964. A loaf of bread costs one shilling (5p). Harold Wilson is Prime Minister of Britain. There are half a million people on the dole; they receive benefit of three pounds seven shillings and sixpence (£3.37½) per week. Four young men calling themselves The Beatles are taking America by storm. Britain is the centre of fashion and pop music. This is what made the Sixties 'The Swinging Sixties'.

Left *Carnaby Street, one of London's most fashionable streets in the Sixties.*

Right *Pop records by British groups were becoming very popular.*

FASHION

Teenagers in the Sixties wanted to dress differently from their parents. Mary Quant was a famous designer who made fashionable, cheap clothes especially for the modern teenager. She opened her first boutique, called 'Bazaar', in the King's Road. People came from all over the world to visit the King's Road and Carnaby Street in London.

Teenage girls wore miniskirts, sling-back shoes in patent leather and skinny-rib jumpers. Dresses were worn short and were either called 'shifts' (straight up and down) or 'dolly dresses' (like little girls' dresses). Teenage boys copied the Beatles' style of dress, with their collarless jackets and button-down shirts. Bell-bottoms, and later clogs, caftans and maxiskirts could be bought at London's bustling street markets.

During the Sixties people liked to experiment with many different 'looks'. There was the 'gangster look' (after the film *Bonnie and Clyde*) and the 'Russian look' (after the film *Dr Zhivago*). The 'little-boy-lost look' was also popular. Girls often wore trousers and waistcoats with large, kipper-shaped ties (designed by a Mr. Fish!). At one time the 'wet look' became fashionable, when PVC mackintoshes were all the rage.

There was also a craze for black-and-white clothes. This idea came from the new 'pop art', which used patterns of black and white to trick the eyes. Towards the end of the Sixties many people adopted the hippy look.

Below and opposite *The two couples on the left are dressed in early-Sixties styles; the hippy look (right) became popular later.*

HAIRSTYLES AND MAKE-UP

In the early years of the Sixties, teenage girls backcombed their hair to make it stand high on top of their heads. Sometimes they added false hair pieces. The Beatles haircut was very popular for a while with teenage boys. Then the unisex hairstyle became fashionable. Girls and boys wore their hair cropped short. Vidal Sassoon was a famous hairdresser who started this fashion. He cut hair in a wedge shape. Later on, when the hippy movement influenced fashion, hair was worn long by both boys and girls.

At the beginning of the decade teenage girls liked to wear very pale lipstick and dark, heavy 'peel-off' eyeliner. False eyelashes were often worn or even painted on the face.

Twiggy, who made her reputation from modelling Sixties styles.

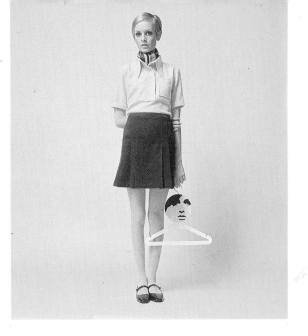

Twiggy, a famous fashion model, became well known for this style. Face painting became popular for a time in the mid-Sixties. Teenagers would draw flowers and hearts on their cheeks and forehead as a form of decoration. A new 'look' in make-up was introduced by Mary Quant the fashion designer. She chose dark, plummy colours for the lips and eyes. False fingernails were also used. These cleverly covered up bitten or broken nails.

Below and opposite *The short haircuts of the early Sixties were replaced by longer styles later in the decade.*

MUSIC

Music played an important part in the life of a teenager during the Sixties. British groups were very popular. The Beatles were by far the most famous group. Teenagers all over the world bought their records. Wherever the Beatles went, crowds of screaming girls followed, calling out 'John! Paul! George! Ringo!' – the names of their idols.

The first discotheque in Britain opened in London in 1961. It was a new kind of dance hall. The idea came from France. Instead of live bands providing the music, disc jockeys selected and played records through stereo loudspeakers. People experimented with new styles of dancing. The most famous dance from that time is the 'Twist'.

Many open-air pop concerts were given in the Sixties. The most famous was at Woodstock, just outside New York. Half a million fans came for three days to listen to the music provided by live bands like The Who, who were famous for smashing their instruments and equipment on stage in the excitement.

Some of the pop stars of the Sixties, like Cliff Richard, The Rolling Stones, Stevie Wonder and Diana Ross are still performing successfully today.

Gradually throughout the Sixties a change of mood came over the kind of music that was being played. This was because of the hippy movement. The music became more 'laid back', which is the phrase the hippies used to mean relaxed and dreamy.

Left *Discotheques gradually began to replace live bands in nightclubs.*

Right *The Beatles attracted screaming fans whenever they appeared.*

The Media

In 1961 three-quarters of all the families in Britain had a television. Most teenagers spent several hours watching television every day. By 1967 colour television was available for the first time.

Teenagers enjoyed watching *Dr Who*, *Top of the Pops* and *Blue Peter*. *Juke Box Jury* was also a great favourite. During this show, a panel of famous people reviewed the latest pop songs and decided if they thought they would be hits or not. *That Was The Week That Was* had an audience of twelve million. It was a lively show that looked back jokingly at the week's events.

Teenagers now watched television instead of going to the cinema. Hundreds of cinemas had to close down.

Juke Box Jury *brought pop music on to television.*

Some teenagers, however, were tempted to go and see Sean Connery as James Bond. Pop stars made films too. The Beatles made the highly successful film *Help!* Thousands of teenagers went to see Cliff Richard in *Summer Holiday*.

Teenagers wanted to listen to continuous (non-stop) pop music. This was only produced by the illegal pirate radio stations. But then the BBC changed all this and set up a new channel on the radio. Their new Radio One programme employed disc jockeys like Tony Blackburn and Kenny Everett who had begun their careers working for the pirate stations.

Many of the comics and magazines which are on sale today were started in the Sixties. These include the fashion magazine *19* and other magazines like *Time Out* and *Private Eye*. A copy of the Dandy cost threepence (just over 1p) in 1963. There were illegal 'underground' magazines too. *Oz* was perhaps the most famous. It was started in 1966.

Tony Blackburn, the pirate radio disc jockey who moved to Radio One.

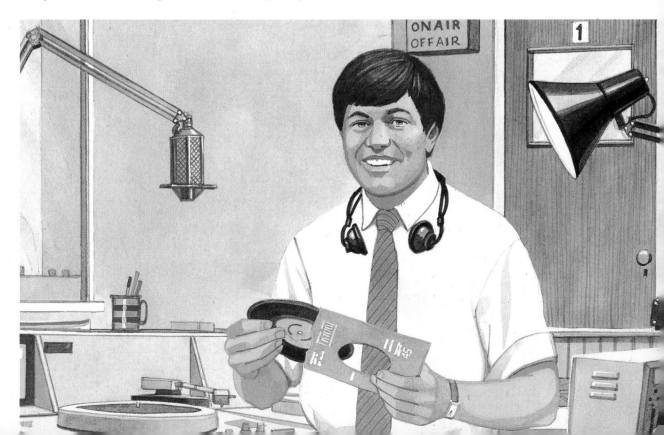

MODS, ROCKERS AND HIPPIES

In the Sixties, teenagers liked to belong to large groups which had their own fashions, music and ideas. The three main groups were the mods, the rockers and the hippies.

Fights between mods and rockers at seaside resorts were reported with panic in many sections of the media.

Mods dressed in the latest fashion. They wore parkas, which were khaki coats, to keep their smart clothes clean. Their hair was short and neat. Mods rode Lambretta or Vespa scooters. They decorated them with mirrors, badges and stickers. They listened to 'modernist' music and enjoyed dancing in nightclubs.

A rocker's image was tough. Rockers liked rock-and-roll music, as their name suggests. Both boys and girls wore metal-studded leather jackets and scruffy jeans. They rode around on powerful motorbikes.

Mods liked to play in amusement arcades, sit in cafés or walk along the beach at seaside towns on Bank Holiday weekends. These seaside towns were often the scenes of violence as mods clashed with rockers. Deck chairs and bottles were thrown.

Once a teenager was killed.

The hippy movement started in America. Hippies were against war, especially the Vietnam War that the Americans were fighting through most of the Sixties. They believed in 'peace and love' and sharing. Hippies grew their hair long, wore colourful jewellery and clothes that were made out of soft, embroidered materials. Magical, ancient places, like Stonehenge, became fashionable meeting places for the hippies.

FREE TIME

Teenagers in the Sixties sometimes went to dance halls in the evenings. Then coffee and milk bars installed jukeboxes which played the more popular music that the teenagers wanted to hear. These became favourite meeting places where teenagers could buy soft drinks, smoke and chat. Soon 'beat clubs' started to open. The most famous was in Liverpool and was called the Cavern. It was in a basement and it was here that the Beatles first played. Teenagers also liked to meet in pubs, where they could listen to the live music. The Yardbirds and the Animals often played at the local pub before they became famous.

In the Sixties teenage workers had more holiday time than ever before. They also had more money to spend. Cheap package holidays, especially to Spain, became very popular.

More teenagers than ever before owned cars. Millions of pounds were spent by the government on new motorways, car parks, by-passes and parking meters to help with the new flood of traffic. Teenagers were now able to travel all over Britain in their free time, seeing friends and new places. Those without cars were often very adventurous, going further afield. They travelled thousands of miles with very little money, sometimes hitching as far as India.

Left   *Many groups in the Sixties started off playing in small 'beat clubs'.*

Right   *Coffee bars were popular meeting places for the young.*

SPORT

In the Sixties many teenagers became interested in outdoor activities like camping, rambling, climbing and pony trekking. A range of water sports became popular. Teenagers took their surfboards to surf off the coast of Cornwall and Devon. The numbers who took up sailing doubled and the number of canoe clubs tripled. Teenagers also liked to go rowing on rivers and lakes.

Many new leisure and sports centres opened. Here the teenagers swam, played tennis, badminton, squash and table tennis.

Surfing, like bowling, came to Britain from America.

Bowling alleys provided sport and a place for young people to meet.

Tenpin bowling was a craze that was brought to England from America. The biggest bowling centre was at Dagenham in Essex. It had twenty-four lanes. Teenagers went there to play, or watch from the comfort of the coffee bars. But this was a craze that never really caught on in a big way.

Fewer teenagers in the Sixties went to live matches. Instead they often watched football, cricket or tennis on the television. Sporting heroes like the footballer George Best or the world heavyweight boxing champion Cassius Clay (later Muhammad Ali) had the same sort of following as pop stars. Many British teenagers dreamed of becoming football heroes, especially after the England team won the World Cup in 1966 at Wembley Stadium.

FOOD AND DRINK

Convenience foods became very popular in the Sixties. These are foods that are frozen, tinned or dried. Teenagers enjoyed foods like fish fingers and instant puddings. Everyone wanted to spend less time on shopping, cooking and eating. One reason for this was that far more women than ever before were going out to work.

New Chinese and Indian take-aways competed with fish and chip shops for business.

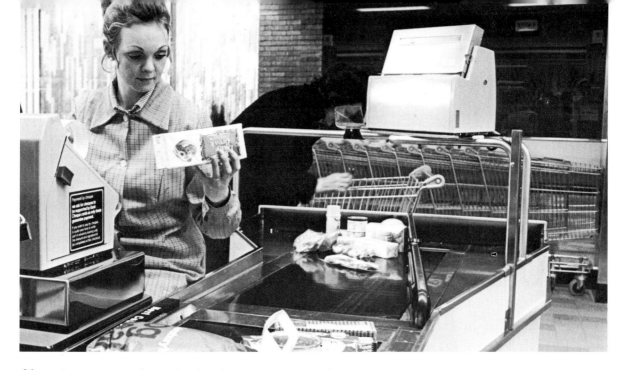

Shopping was made easier by the new supermarkets.

Supermarkets started opening at a tremendous rate. There were only one hundred in 1956. This increased to three thousand by 1967! A teenager shopping in one of these new supermarkets might have bought a jar of peanut butter for two shillings (10p), a packet of biscuits for two shillings and sixpence (12½p), a cake mix for two shillings and fourpence (11p) and a tin of Carnation milk for two shillings and eightpence (13½p).

Teenagers began to take an interest in foreign food and recipes. People used more garlic in their cooking. They bought exotic fruit and vegetables, like aubergines and avocadoes, from the greengrocer.

Hundreds of new restaurants opened serving French, Italian, Chinese, Turkish and Greek dishes. But eating out was too expensive for some teenagers. Instead they went to the new take-away restaurants. There were plenty of kebab houses and Indian and Chinese take-aways with cheap menus which they could easily afford.

Fish and chip shops were still popular, however, and every town centre soon had its own plushly decorated steakhouse. In pubs more people drank wine, and real ale became rare. It was replaced by the fizzier keg beer that was easier to make.

THE GENERATION GAP

Many teenagers in the Sixties felt unhappy about where they lived. The high-rise buildings that were built at that time destroyed the friendliness that teenagers had found in small neighbourhoods. There was no community spirit and the bad living conditions put strains on family life. Many teenagers criticized their parents and people in authority. This was known as the 'Generation Gap'.

Some teenagers were looking for new and different experiences. They tried to escape what they thought was the boredom of their everyday lives by copying their pop star idols. Some of these were known to experiment with drugs, often with very sad results. Brian Jones of The Rolling Stones was one of the pop stars who died as a result of taking drugs.

Some teenagers used illegal drugs called amphetamines to make them feel energetic. These drugs had names which made them sound more attractive than they really were, like 'Purple Hearts', 'French Blues' and 'Black Bombers'. They cost about sixpence (2½p) each and were bought at nightclubs.

By 1968 it was thought that perhaps as many as three hundred thousand teenagers and adults might be experimenting with another drug called marijuana (also known as grass, pot and hash). Another very dangerous drug which was used was called LSD. This affected the way people saw things.

Many hippy teenagers refused to live the same kind of life as their parents. They left home and squatted in broken-down houses in towns.

Some hippies wanted to get back to nature. They 'dropped out' of ordinary life altogether and lived in communes in the country. They refused to work for big firms like their parents. Instead they made and sold their own goods. By the end of the Sixties there were several thousand communes in America and about fifty in England.

Opposite *The 'alternative' lifestyles of many teenagers led to arguments with their parents.*

AT SCHOOL AND COLLEGE

In the Sixties nearly all children took an examination at the age of eleven. This was to decide whether they went on to a grammar school or to a secondary modern school after leaving primary school. Teenagers who went to the grammar school took Ordinary (O) Level and Advanced (A) Level examinations. Some went on to colleges and a few went to universities.

Teenagers who went to the secondary modern schools took the usual subjects plus more practical subjects like carpentry and cookery. Most left school at fifteen and went straight to their first job. Some went on to colleges to learn other skills.

Much of the 'pop art' of the Sixties was created by young people studying at colleges and art schools. Imagination and creativity were considered very important in the Sixties and began to be encouraged in schools.

By 1964 many people thought that all teenagers should be educated in a school they called a 'comprehensive'. They believed that it was fairer that children of mixed abilities should be taught together. In this new kind of school they wanted the lessons to be more enjoyable and imaginative. Some schools would no

Boys and girls were usually kept apart in grammar schools.

longer insist that teenagers had to wear uniforms.

At the end of the Sixties many schools were beginning to change over to this new comprehensive system of education.

25

PROTEST!

The year 1968 was a year of student protest in universities in America, West Germany, France, Japan, Italy and Britain.

Students in France led a huge demonstration through Paris hoping to force a change of government. They seized the university buildings. Factory workers who supported them took over the factories. This action shocked the French government of President de Gaulle but did not succeed in bringing it down.

In America students protested against the Vietnam War that America was fighting during the Sixties. There were often battles between the students and the police.

The Sixties were also a time of peaceful protest marches. In America in 1963, protesters organized by Martin Luther King, a black leader, marched on Washington DC. They wanted black people in America to be treated fairly.

The Campaign for Nuclear Disarmament (CND) held an Easter march each year in the Sixties. Thousands of people took part, making their way from Aldermaston in Berkshire to London in order to protest about nuclear weapons.

Pop stars like Bob Dylan and Donovan sang protest songs against war, hunger and poverty. One anti-war song composed by Bob Dylan is called *A Hard Rain's A Gonna Fall*. It warns us about what it would be like if a nuclear bomb was dropped.

Left   *Hippy lifestyles were in themselves a kind of protest.*

Right   *Peace protesters place flowers in soldiers' guns.*

AT WORK

There were only half a million unemployed people in Britain during the Sixties. This meant that teenagers leaving school had little trouble in finding a job. Most teenagers left school at fifteen and went to work straight away. In 1961 a young man's average earnings were about £15 a week. By 1969 these had risen to £24.

Although British workers were earning more they were not producing more. Five typists at a firm in Surrey offered to work an extra half-hour every day free of charge. They said they wanted to 'Back Britain' – to make Britain great again. This started the 'I'm Backing Britain' campaign. Everyone was encouraged to buy British-made goods.

Fashion-conscious youngsters were keen to work in the new boutiques.

The Union Jack flag appeared on everything, from tea towels to Rolls Royce cars.

Teenagers liked to work in boutiques, where they could see the latest fashions as soon as they arrived. Girls often went straight from school to work in one of the new supermarkets.

Large factories each provided jobs for thousands of people.

Many teenagers worked in factories or on production lines that mass-produced popular mini cars or electrical goods. People started to worry that new machinery might one day take over their jobs.

29

LOOKING BACK

The Sixties were a time of great energy. The Russians put the first man, Yuri Gagarin, in space. American astronauts landed on the moon in 1969 in the Apollo 11 spacecraft. Satellites beamed television programmes around the world. Professor Christiaan Barnard performed the first heart transplant.

During the Sixties more people owned cars, washing machines, fridges and televisions than before. But it was also a time of poor housing, rising crime and drug-taking among young people.

Most importantly it was the first time that teenagers and young people played such a big part in changing the way adults thought. Young people led the way in fashion and music. They said what they thought about war and injustice. The Sixties were a lively and exciting time to be a teenager.

An astronaut, a satellite, the mini, pop records and Dr Who: *just some of the images of the Sixties.*

GLOSSARY

Boutique A small shop which sells fashionable clothes.

Caftan A loose dress with long, wide sleeves.

Campaign for Nuclear Disarmament A movement which wants all countries to stop producing nuclear weapons.

Communes Groups of families or people living together and sharing possessions.

Dole Money given by the government to people who are out of work.

Hitching Travelling by getting free lifts from drivers.

LSD Lysergic acid diethylamide, a dangerous drug which makes the user see things which are not there.

Marijuana The dried leaves and flowers of the hemp plant smoked as a drug.

Maxiskirts Very long skirts to the ankle.

Package holidays Holidays offered by travel agents in which they take care of all the travelling, eating and sleeping arrangements. This is included in the total price.

Pirate radio stations Radio stations run by people illegally.

PVC Shiny plastic material.

Squatted When people have occupied a house, usually empty, that does not belong to them.

Unisex This refers to clothes or hairstyles which can be worn by either boys or girls.

MORE BOOKS TO READ

Susan Cleeve, *Growing up in the Swinging Sixties* (Wayland, 1980).

Nathaniel Harris, *The Sixties* (Macdonald, 1975).

Nigel Hunter, *Martin Luther King* (Wayland, 1985).

Vanora Leigh, *John Lennon* (Wayland, 1986). This gives you more information about the Beatles.

INDEX

Picture acknowledgements

The publishers would like to thank the following for supplying the photographs used in this book: Picturepoint 4, 10, 16; Popperfoto 9; Topham 24, 28; Wayland Picture Library 21, 26.